100 WAYS TO BECOME A SUCCESSFUL TEENAGER

100 Ways to Become a Successful Teenager

A Successful Teenager

Teen Success Series Volume II

"This book is practical, effective,
gives examples and speaks with motivation!"

Yvonne Brooks

iUniverse, Inc.

New York   Lincoln   Shanghai

100 Ways to Become a Successful Teenager
Teen Success Series Volume II

iUniverse books may be ordered through booksellers or by contacting:

iUniverse
2021 Pine Lake Road, Suite 100
Lincoln, NE 68512
www.iuniverse.com
1-800-Authors (1-800-288-4677)

ISBN-13: 978-0-595-37681-0 (pbk)
ISBN-13: 978-0-595-82063-4 (ebk)
ISBN-10: 0-595-37681-9 (pbk)
ISBN-10: 0-595-82063-8 (ebk)

Printed in the United States of America

This book is dedicated to teenagers who struggle with family, health, emotions, education and social stressors. I confess that this book will bring more peace, contentment, and joy to your lives, and no negative plans that is formed against those who read and apply the principles in this will come to past.

Special dedication goes to Parkman Plus Students, Aneeka, Rick, Sako, Trey, Juan, Gladys, Stephanie, Amit, Karlene, Cassandra, Evan, Nicole, Christie, Robert and Michael. Your special love and kindness gave me the strength to release this book, which will be read by millions of young adults nationwide. Wishing you the best mentally, physically and spiritually. God Bless!

I love you all!

Contents

Introduction

As this book took form, I realized that it was going to take a great deal of sacrifice, commitment and dedication. It is a privilege to write this book. Over the years, I have come to appreciate the many trials and mistakes that it took to prepare and shape my destiny. As a young adult, I was always looking outside myself for answers. I had no concept of what it meant to trust my intuitions. I gave up easily whenever I made mistakes. I tried to please everyone and failed.

Overcoming my struggles slowly and patiently gave me the strength and confidence that I needed to succeed. Implementing the tips written in this book, with trial and error, was the greatest gift I gave myself.

My hunger for success has led me to read many books on the subject, which inspired me to become a writer for young adults. I have spent the last fifteen years researching and developing a series of leadership programs designed to empower young adults and their parents. Some of these programs are currently being taught online, at public libraries, schools and churches throughout the United States.

As you read this book, millions of teenagers are struggling internally and externally with issues and situations that eventually affect the outcome of their grades and their future. Issues such as stress, anxiety, fear, procrastination, anger and a negative home environment are just a few of the things that affect teens daily. The information in this book is a guideline for teenagers, and designed to increase their success level. By reading this book, teenagers will be exposed to one hundred powerful tips for success. Many successful leaders have made peace with their daily struggles in order to improve their effectiveness and strategies for success. The tips in this book are teen friendly and can be implemented immediately to help young adults cope more effectively with daily stressors, and, thus, become more successful in all areas of their life. Remember, the key word is **IMPLEMENT**. Throughout the world teenagers are longing for encouragement from others. Make an effort to share some of these success tips with other fellow teens.

Teen Leadership Assessment

Write "Yes" or "No" to the following questions:

1) I am financially prepared for college   _____
2) I have written down my high school & college goals   _____
3) I am in control of my anger   _____
4) I have a Teen Financial Portfolio in place   _____
5) I am very clear about my future   _____
6) I am self-motivated   _____
7) I am always confident about my leadership abilities   _____
8) I take full responsibility for all my behavior   _____
9) I am a good listener   _____
10) I forgive those who hurt me   _____

If you have answered "**no**" to one or more questions, use this book as a guide towards improving your overall mental and physical abilities. Use it as a tool to brush up on skills that you forgot you had. If these questions do not apply to you, I would like to congratulate you and wish you much success as you share this book with close friends and family members.

Section One

Family Success Tips

In 2001, youth suicide was the third leading cause of death in the United States among youths aged 13–18 years, accounting for 11% of deaths in this age group. In 2003, approximately one in twelve high school students in the United States reported attempting suicide during the preceding 12 months.

Potential indicators of suicide risk such as, expressions of suicidal thoughts, recent social stressors, and substance abuse use were common among victims. The finding that 22% of students who carried out such violence took their own lives indicates that a sizeable proportion of lethal school-associated violence was self-directed. In addition, the finding that approximately one in four suicide victims injured or killed someone else immediately before their suicide suggests an overlap between risk for committing school-associated homicide and risk for suicide. (MMW Weekly, June 11, 2004/53(22); 476-478)

The family is a divinely inspired institution that came into existence to provide support, safety and comfort to all members. For many teenagers the family represents a safe haven, for others the family represent a battlefield. The family was never created to push teenagers away or make them feel unwanted. It was created to empower, uplift and provide tools for children, who would at a later date, contribute back, exactly that which was poured into them. I hope the teens that read this section of the book, will find some comfort and know that we love, cherish and adore them. I beg forgiveness for all the adults who have hurt, insulted or created any uneasiness in a young adult's life. I desire that young adults will be more patient with their families, and never give up trying to get the help and support needed to succeed in life.

SUCCESS TIP #1

Respect Your Parents

Respecting your parents is at the top of the list for teenagers who are emotionally strong and successful. Parents represent an authority where children receive their blessings. Respecting your parents will bring goodness, peace of mind, financial prosperity and healthy relationships with others. Always be kind to your parents, the rewards are far greater than when you choose to be disobedient and unkind.

Activity:

- Celebrate this week as "Being Kind to My Parent Week."
- Introduce your parents to your school counselor.
- Pray for your parents to be more patient with you.

SUCCESS TIP #2

Create A Mission Statement For Your Life

Ask yourself these questions: What do I stand for in life? What are my goals after high school? Where do I see myself in the future? What do I really want out of life? What dreams do I want to experience with my family? The answers to all of these questions will bring you one step closer to your mission in life.

All you need to do is take action consistently until you achieve your mission. Do not waste your time in an area that will not bring you closer to your mission. Do not wait five years to create a mission statement. Do it now!

Activity:

- Create a personal mission statement for your life.
  (Example: My mission in life is to be more patient, loving, and kind; so as to become a responsible and effective leader, mentor, parent and friend.)
- Cross-reference your daily activities with your mission statement to make sure that they always match.
- Eliminate all activities that do not support your mission.

SUCCESS TIP #3

Work On Your Attitude

Your attitude, negative or positive, is your highest form of communication when dealing with others. The results you receive from family and friends daily are based simply on your attitude. Check yourself at the end of the day; if you are getting a lot of negative attention, begin working on your attitude to bring about the positive results that you desire. If you get a lot of positive results, congratulate yourself and repeat the same behavior in order to receive more of the same.

Activity:

- Take inventory of all the areas that you are accepting less than your highest potential.
- Begin to seek out mentors who will empower you towards achieving your highest goals.
- Spend time with motivated teenagers who are successful leaders.

SUCCESS TIP #4

Have Compassion

Having compassion for family members, who are experiencing difficulties with a divorce, or lack of finance to take care of the bills, is an excellent attribute of a successful teenager. There are many parents, teachers, counselors and mentors who are waiting for teens to have more compassion towards them. Some parents struggle as a single parent, some teachers struggle with being paid below the poverty line. What these individuals need more than anything, is a teenager who has a heart to see the pain and not add to it, but have the desire to show more compassion and love.

Activity:

- Create a list of individuals that you need to show more compassion towards.
- Create a list of things you can do for each individual.
- Spend the week sharing more love and compassion to everyone.

SUCCESS TIP #5

Clean Your Room

Do you keep your room messy? Do you wear dirty clothes the next day? Do you have your school papers all over the floor and out of order? Is your mind filled with clutter? Do you look like a mess when you go to school? Do your parents tell you to pick up after yourself? Are you a teenager who just has too much clutter in your life? If you answered "Yes" to any of these questions, I am excited about sharing this information with you. Clutter is a sign of disrespect and irresponsibility towards oneself. Teenagers who keep their environment clean are usually positive, have more energy and have healthier relationships than teenagers who surround themselves with clutter.

Activity:

- Write down your feelings before you begin this activity.
- Clean your room spotless.
- Arrange your books, clothes, toys etc.
- Wear clean clothes daily.
- Record in your journal how you felt after completing this activity.

SUCCESS TIP #6

Give Out Lots Of Compliments

Giving out lots of compliments builds strong self-esteem in other people, which in turn builds your self-esteem. Give compliments that are genuine and true. Compliment your parents or guardian on how great he or she looks, or on something they have done that you are proud of. Compliment your family members, friends, neighbors and all those you admire. The amount of compliments you give out shows how much self-esteem you possess.

Activity:

- Give out one hundred compliments this week.
- Write a letter to your parents complimenting them.
- Practice being more patient with others this week.

SUCCESS TIP #7

Keep Your Mouth Clean

For most teenagers, cursing is cool and hip. What most teens fail to realize is, a filthy mouth equals a filthy mind. This behavior can cause confusion for many teens. It is impossible to serve two masters. Oil and water will always separate when poured into the same glass. Successful teenagers speak good things with their mouths, and leave filthy talk to others who are still learning about self-respect and honoring themselves.

Activity:

* Do a survey with your friends to see if you have a filthy or clean mouth.
* Make a promise to yourself that you will clean up all filthy language for the rest of the year.
* Take notice of how much your grades and quality of friendships have improved.

SUCCESS TIP #8

Tell Others That They Are Important To You

Do not wait until it is too late to let your family and those around you know just how important they are to you. On a daily basis, share your true feelings with those who are with you now. Do not wait until they have moved away; passed on; or no longer in your life because of your inability to share love. Take a bold step and let them know that each day is a special day for you, just because of their relationship and love.

Activity:

- Create a list of ten individuals who are currently in your life.
- Contact each one and let them know just how much you love and adore them.
- Celebrate your ability to follow through with this activity with a friend.

SUCCESS TIP #9

Quit Complaining

It is amazing to see the amount of teenagers who constantly complain about parents, teachers, homework, friends, and everything that was meant to provide support and comfort. Complaining is another way of being ungrateful. It is not an attribute of a successful teenager. Instead of complaining, try caring for someone in need.

Activity:

• Send a Gift Basket to a shelter for Abused Children.

• Donate food to a local food bank.

• Buy lunch for someone in need this week.

SUCCESS TIP #10

Manage Your Money With Confidence

Money management skills are one of many necessary attributes that successful teenagers embrace. Overspending, using parents like an ATM machine, begging, borrowing, stealing, are not money management traits possessed by a successful teenager. Successful teenagers work very hard with a mentor at creating a teen financial portfolio that will earn interest, while in middle and high school, so as to produce wealth before entering college.

Activity:

- Select a financial mentor.
- Meet with your mentor one hour monthly for five year.
- Contact the author of this book to receive a free teen financial checklist by age group.
- Share this powerful tip with a friend.

SUCCESS TIP #11

Show Affection

Allow time in your busy schedule to give and receive lots of love and affection from your family members without limitations. It is important that you give affection without looking for something in return. This is called manipulation. Show affection because you really enjoy doing it, not because you need a cell phone or a new video game. Your affection must be unconditional. For example, give out lots of hugs or smiles; tell your parents "I love you;" or share with your brothers/sisters personal information about your day. Sharing with others will bring success, making it easier to experience joy and peace throughout the day.

Activity:

- Get up early on the weekend and clean the house for your parents.
- Tell your parents just how much you love them today.
- Spend an afternoon at the park with your grandparents.
- Use your phone time to play hide and seek with your siblings.

SUCCESS TIP #12

Treat Others The Way You Would Like To Be Treated

Do not treat anyone less than the way you would like to be treated. When teens respect and care for themselves in ways that support personal development, they will begin to treat family and others the same way. When teens possess low self-esteem, as well as, a negative outlook and attitude, they will treat family and others accordingly. Even though others may disrespect you, remember that they are only letting you know just how awful they feel about themselves. Respect them for sharing their darkness, but never allow what they say or do to bring you to their level. Teens have a lot of goodness to offer their family and friends. Use it well!

Activity:

- Go out of your way this week to treat your family like royalty.
- Dare them to return the favor.
- Do the same for yourself.

SUCCESS TIP #13

Love Yourself Unconditionally

Give yourself the highest unconditional love you can give. Spend the time to improve the personal attention you give to yourself. Do not wait for family or friends to show you love first. Make it your responsibility to improve your personal relationship. It is OK to love YOU, even if no one else notices how special you are.

Love is such a powerful tool that we all need. So many teenagers have there own interpretation of what love is. Unconditional love is not "love me today, hate me and the world tomorrow". Unconditional love is "Love me today and others forever," no strings attached. The kind of love that I would like to recommend is one without restrictions or demands. Go out of your way to show more unconditional love to yourself, especially when you make the biggest mistakes.

Activity:

- Write a love letter to yourself about how much you adore and appreciate who you truly are.
- Write a love letter from yourself about how much you are loved.
- Pamper yourself at the spa this week.

SUCCESS TIP #14

Honor Your Self

Respect is earned by honoring one's self first, then, sharing the same techniques with others. Get into the habit of being more respectful to your family, friends, teachers, and authority figures over you. Respect is a reward given freely by those who reflect the level of honor they give to themselves. Instead of getting angry when someone disrespects you, check to see if they are reflecting your current behavior of self-honor.

Activity:

- Honor yourself and others this week.
- Go out of your way to honor a senior citizen this week.
- Review the results at the end of two weeks.

SUCCESS TIP #15

Whisper A Prayer Everyday

Pray and mediate about your present situation. A simple prayer or time alone in silence can fill you up with energy that can boost personal strength and confidence. Pray that goodness, perfect peace, wealth and success come to your family, friends and loved ones. Pray for teenagers who are without parents, food and shelter around the world. Pray for your school district, teachers, and counselors that they will be kind and supportive to all children, no matter what race, culture or religion. Pray that more teenagers will care about the needy and the poor.

Activity:

- Go out of your way this week to pray for your parents.
- Spend time in silence giving thanks for teenagers who will be graduating from high school this year.
- Pray for teens that are bound by drugs and alcohol to be set free.
- Give up sugar for one day annually, in remembrance of children with aids and cancer.

SUCCESS TIP #16

Give To Others

The ability to give is a powerful attribute many successful teenagers love to practice. Giving gifts from your heart is encouraged because the rewards are far greater than giving a gift with expectation. The gift of giving could be your time, your friendship, taking someone out to lunch and paying for it, or donating money to a worthy cause. Many successful teenagers have developed an annual gift-giving plan. A gift-giving plan teaches teens how to show compassion and love for their friends, family and the community at an early age.

Activity:

- Create an annual gift-giving plan.
- Create a list of individuals that you would like to give more to this year.
- List individuals by date of birth.
- Take pictures of each person (create a scrap page for each month and add to your scrapbook.)
- Mail birthday cards and gifts at appropriate time.
- Celebrate!

SUCCESS TIP #17

Improve Your Relationships

Knowing how to communicate effectively with your family and others is very important. Knowing what you want, where you are going and what you desire in life is very necessary. Being honest with your relationships is one way of improving them. Tell the truth always when you feel violated. Being respectful and kind is another way. There are endless ways to learn how to improve your relationship with family members and others, simply apply one of these techniques daily in order to avoid neglect.

Activity:

- Identify your likes and dislikes.
- Work on ways to improve your relationship with your dislikes.
- Share your likes with your family this week.
- Recommend that your family support you with one item from your list.

SUCCESS TIP #18

Know That You Are Blessed

Putting yourself down when you make mistakes is not necessary. You have come a long way with your self-development, and should be at the point where you know and believe that you are blessed. Blessed with your studies, blessed with a loving family, blessed with an awesome teacher and blessed with the best friends ever. Be proud of yourself and look forward to a great year.

Activity:

• Catch yourself criticizing your abilities and "STOP."

• Create a list of all your blessings.

• Remember to always thank those who bless you each day.

• Thank a family member who encouraged you this year.

SUCCESS TIP #19

Lift Your Head High

Lift your head high knowing that you are ready and capable of experiencing personal growth and success with your family, friends and school. Do not put pressure on yourself to complete all these suggestions immediately; you will need time to implement the success tips from this book. Again, if the results you wanted were not achieved, simply tell yourself that you will do better next time. When you pressure yourself to be the best without allowing room to fail or make mistakes, you are actually setting yourself up for disaster. Remember be gentle!

Activity:

- Practice walking and looking straight ahead, (not on the ground.)
- Look people in the eye when they speak to you.
- Give full attention to your family goals.

SUCCESS TIP #20

Take Charge Of Your Life

Take a stand for yourself. When teens refuse to take charge of their lives, they make it easier for others to pull them into directions that are sometimes unpleasant and unsafe. Make your own decisions; stop asking someone else to decide for you. Learn to depend on YOU more.

Activity:

- Create a list of things that you allow others to make decisions on.
- Review each item on the list and take a stand for each one by yourself.
- Ask a parent to assist with this activity.

SUCCESS TIP #21

Cancel All Pity Parties

Self-pity is not our friend; it is our enemy. Entertaining private mental parties about the form of discipline your parent used, or crying yourself to sleep because you failed an exam are sure ways to fail at life. Look yourself in the mirror and tell yourself that you are strong. Let self-pity know that you will never give up.

Your situation will only last for as long as you allow it. Pick yourself up, get a mentor immediately, see a counselor, and do something about every situation that tries to steal your joy and happiness. Everyone experiences disappointment from time to time, however, it is up to you to determine how long it will last, and whether you will deal with it positively or negatively.

Activity:

- Create a list of things that you are currently inviting to your pity parties.
- Ask a mentor or a counselor to help with finding solutions.
- Implement the solutions for each problem immediately.
- Celebrate your success of canceling all your pity parties.
- Send a thank you note to your mentor or counselor.
- Take yourself out for lunch. You deserve it!

SUCCESS TIP #22

Reverse Negative Labels

Negativity is designed to rob one of his/her current and future successes. Limit the amount of negative programming you give yourself and the amount you allow yourself to receive from others. Be more alert about personal negative messages, such as "How could I be so stupid?" or "I knew it wouldn't work!" Take mental notes regarding the labels others speak into your life, such as "You don't have what it takes to get into university," or "You will never get out of special education classes."

Negative messages are the reason we fail without knowing why. Most of these messages come from labels that were spoken into our lives from parents, teachers, babysitters, friends, or strangers. Although many teenagers want to become successful, they have a hard time achieving this task, when others speak negativity or death to their dreams or goals. Watch your response and reaction when others make negative statements regarding your life. Be sure to keep it positive. Repeat this exercise until you break the habit of negative programming.

Activity:

- Create a list of negative messages that you repeat to yourself daily.
- Write a positive message for each item on your list.
- Share this assignment with your parent.
- Give thanks for the person who introduced you to this book.

SUCCESS TIP #23

Take Authority

Taking authority is simply taking control. There are many things that we do not have control over, but there are a lot of things in our lives that we refuse to take responsibility for. Many teens have the authority to control their behaviors. Teens have authority over how they respond to situations and how long they allow themselves to stay in a situation. The issue with most teens is that they are unaware that they have this authority. If you have not heard the news yet, let me enlighten you to a true fact that "All Teens Have The Authority To Succeed." To access this authority, teens must first receive the message that they have the authority then begin taking positive control in every area of their lives.

Activity:

- Create a list of all the things you do not believe you have control over.
- Sit with a parent or trusted friend to review your list.
- Ask for advice about creating an action plan for each item on your list.
- Implement your plan immediately.

SUCCESS TIP #24

Do Not Blame Others For Your Problems

Blaming family members and others for your problems will only lower your self-esteem. Get into the habit of taking personal responsibility for everything you do. Learn how to be honest with yourself and about your feelings.

Hiding behind others from problems will only teach teens how *not* to be truthful and honest. Being honest comes with consequences, but these consequences will teach you how to become a better teenager and ultimately, a better person.

Activity:

- Allow yourself to make mistakes.
- Treat yourself when you mess up.
- Speak kindly to yourself especially when you fail.
- Remember that each failure leads one step closer to success.

SUCCESS TIP #25

Solve Problems With Ease

Step One: First, decide what the problem is

Step Two: Write down the problem

Step Three: Write down 10 solutions to the problem

Step Four: Create an action plan for step three

Step Five: Evaluate the results from step four

Step Six: Repeat Steps four and five until the problem is solved to your satisfaction

Step Seven: Share technique and Celebrate with family members!

Section Two

Health & Emotion Success Tips

Teenagers never have health or emotional problems, right? Wrong! Teenagers not only can and do encounter unhealthy lifestyles and emotional problems; they also struggle with the advice given to them on how to take better care of themselves.

Balance and control are necessary for good emotions and health. When teens are out of sync, they cannot do their best. All teenagers need a balance in the following categories: family, health, education, social, financial, spiritual, dreams and community. If one of these areas is out of balance, the others are affected also.

Teens do not have to allow their health and emotions to take control over their lives. Issues such as depression, obesity and loneliness, are just a few of the many stressors that many teens have a hard time with daily. When teens get overwhelmed and cannot find solutions themselves, they should know that help is available through a variety of sources, including the medical professions, family members and friends.

I know from my heart that the teenagers who read this section will receive easy to apply information, that will lead them one step closer to becoming healthier and emotionally balanced. This is my desire for all.

SUCCESS TIP #26

Get Proper Nutrition

The foods you eat have a lot to do with your learning capabilities. If you feed your brain junk, then the outcome can only be junk. Give your brain a balanced breakfast, lunch and dinner. Do not skip meals and stay away from diets.

Missing a meal or dieting will slow down your learning process. It lowers mental energy and your ability to retain information. A can of soda, chips and a chocolate bar are not ingredients of a healthy breakfast. While there is nothing wrong with these foods, you must limit the amount you consume and make sure that you balance it out with lots of fruits, vegetables, chicken, fish, water and so on.

Begin your morning with a big breakfast consisting of high fibers, water, juice, fruits, a protein sandwich or cereal. Always start your morning off on the right track. This means your breakfast should be one of your best meals simply because you are going to have your best day ever.

Activity:

- Monitor your eating habits for one week.
- Make changes to reflect one who is going to have his/her best day ever.
- Read books that encourages healthy and balanced living.

SUCCESS TIP #27

Get Plenty of Rest

Most teenagers need an average of eight to nine hours of sleep within a 24-hour period. Anything over twelve hours usually causes teens to become more tired and lazy. Discipline yourself to get the sleep you need daily without waiting for the moment where you just pass out due to your body giving up.

Your body needs rest in order to repair from the daily wear and tear. Cramming for exams, feeding your brain junk, excess drugs, alcohol and lack of sleep are clear signs that you are not ready to become a successful teenager at this time. Although you might feel like you are getting ahead with these negative behaviors, in the end, these behaviors will lead to failure. Take a look at other teens that are engaged in the same behaviors, and are now in rehab facilities, or in jail for failing at every relationship. Take care of yourself the right way, and watch how much more you'll be able to accomplish in the long run.

Activity:

- Plan to get nine hours of sleep each night.
- Change your bed sheets weekly, (**Wash Them.**)
- Create a peaceful atmosphere for your bedroom.
- Clean out all clutter from your room and closet.

SUCCESS TIP #28

Be Gentle With Yourself

Beating up on yourself because you lack certain leadership skills will not help with becoming a successful teenager. Take great care with your emotions. Be kind to yourself when feeling sad, lonely or depress. Encourage yourself even more when no one is available to speak life to you. Be kind and gentle with your daily assignments. Be clear about your weaknesses (*we all have them*), so that you can work towards improving your experience of personal success annually. Treat yourself with special attention and extra care.

Activity:

- Create a list of things that makes you sad or depress.
- Spend this week analyzing why you have given so much power to the situation.
- Forgive everyone involved with each situation, including you.
- Make peace with each situation.
- Move on with your life with more strength and confidence.
- Ask a mentor to assist you with this exercise.

SUCCESS TIP #29

Learn How To Cope Effectively

Throughout your school term, you will be faced with continuous difficulties, heartaches, disappointments and stressful situations. This is an excellent time to add more books to your personal library. Possessing effective coping skills is a reward. There are hundreds of books, tapes and magazines that share techniques that can assist teens with coping effectively with stress, anger, loss of a pet, or depression.

Activity:

- Register at the website www.youthleadership3000.org to learn about leadership programs for teens.
- Research the Internet for other websites for teens.
- Ask a friend to share his/her coping skills.
- Share your results with your counselor.

SUCCESS TIP #30

Forgive Those Who Hurt You

Forgiving those who hurt you is one of the top one hundred things that teens struggle with daily. The ability to hold on to negative feelings plays a major role in the life of many teenagers who fail at having healthy and caring relationships with others. Unhealthy and negative feelings, when held for a long period of time in the heart, can produce sickness and disease.

Although it may seem much easier to hold onto the pain and hurt inside, the resulting damage to your mind and body are far greater. Forgiving an individual does not mean that you were wrong and they were right. It does not mean that you are a bad person.

Forgiveness clears your mind to move on; it creates character; it says that you are a strong person and that you refuse to allow someone else to control how you feel for the rest of your life. Forgiving others shows just how much you love yourself.

Activity:

- Create a list of people who have hurt you in the past.
- Share the pain with your parent, counselor or trusted friend.
- Invite a group of five friends to your forgiveness party.
- Repeat the names of people on your list that hurt.
- Declare openly that you forgive each person.

- Wish the people on your list many blessings.
- Celebrate your breakthrough with the group.
- Ask your group to share the forgiveness tips with others.

SUCCESS TIP #31

Guard Your Heart

In our world today, excessive violence seems to be at an all time high. Many teenagers are bombarded everyday with violence in the home, on the streets, through television and also at school. Successful teenagers usually work a little harder to achieve this skill because the heart is very sensitive to what it is exposed to.

The way to our hearts is through our eyes and our ears. What we allow ourselves to see and hear goes straight to the heart, and, therefore, what we speak out of our mouth daily is a result of what is in the heart. It is very important to remember this skill for the future. Many teenagers will speak words that are cruel and poisonous. But it is only because of their inability to guard their hearts.

Activity:

- Be on alert this week with what you allow to go into your heart.
- Try this technique for twenty-one days.
- Share the results with family and friends.
- Email your results to me. (ypbrooks@msn.com)

SUCCESS TIP #32

Prepare Yourself Mentally

Mental training is about giving full attention to your life. On a daily basis, teens give out a lot of energy to school, homework, family, friends and the telephone. Making time for mental training thirty minutes a day will send the message that you love and care for yourself just as much as you do all the things you give your energy to daily.

I encourage teens to mental train by listening to uplifting music, reading a book that is empowering or writing a list of daily accomplishments in a diary. Mental training for thirty minutes daily will give teens the extra boost they need to complete a project or to help them stay more focused on their goals. Mental training is about refusing to neglect **YOU**.

Activity:

- Review your success journal for thirty minutes daily.
- Feel free to add more successes to your journal daily.
- Teach a friend how to start his/her own success journal.

SUCCESS TIP #33

Control Your Anger

In a state of anger, we are not capable of making good decisions. Anger is a negative emotion designed to destroy all good, based on your reaction to it. Anger towards family members must be dealt with before it's too late. Uncontrollable anger at times can cause an individual to become close-minded, which could lead one to say or do things that he/she will later regret. When anger comes upon you, take time-out; take 20 deep breaths; count backwards from one hundred; take a walk; meditate; whisper a prayer; exercise; or write down what makes you angry, then work your way through it slowly until you find a solution for your anger.

Activity:

- Create a list of things that makes you angry.
- Take time to come up with five positive solutions per problem.
- Implement your solutions **until** you have achieved complete control over each issue.
- Ask a mentor for assistance.

SUCCESS TIP #34

Believe In Yourself

Lack of self-belief only lowers grades and self-esteem. Lack of belief in our abilities produces confusion, and causes many teens to misjudge him/herself. It is the reason why many teenagers answer incorrectly questions they already knew the answers to. Teens who believe in themselves simply give permission to themselves to be strong in areas where once they felt fearful. If you do not believe in you, no one else will.

Activity:

- Tell five people today just how much you believe in them.
- Purchase a copy of this book and donate it to a friend.
- Tell your parents that you believe in their discipline techniques.

SUCCESS TIP #35

Begin An Exercise Program

If you are not on an exercise program at the moment, begin one today. Start walking, swimming, jogging or some type of aerobics exercise. Invest this quality time in yourself. Exercising will increase energy and retention ability in the classroom. Exercising will also help with coping more effectively with stressful situations. The recommended amount of time is three to five days a week. Invest a minimum of three days weekly to help with improving focus and concentration. You won't regret it!

Activity:

- Make a commitment to experience perfect health.
- Ask a friend to join you in exercising this week.
- Read a book this week on ways to improve your health.

SUCCESS TIP #36

Let Go Of Fear

Skipping classes, neglecting to complete homework are attributes of teenagers who allow fear to control them. This is very unhealthy. Sometimes, fear of becoming a successful teenager and the responsibility of being such a person causes teens to behave in a manner that gives FEAR power over their lives.

Replace fear with self-belief. Start giving yourself credit for your accomplishments, quit skipping classes, stop gossiping about other people's business and implement more positive self-talk. Try to build your confidence one-step at a time. You will eventually see your fears diminish and this will allow you to succeed at whatever you do.

Activity:

- Create a list of your fears.
- Rewrite the opposite of each fear in a positive sentence.
- Review daily with your affirmation cards.

SUCCESS TIP #37

Be Honest With Your Feelings

It is all right to feel depressed, alone, sad, angry or lost. Be honest with what you are feeling when you are feeling it. After you have allowed yourself to be honest, immediately find a solution. Do not entertain a "poor me" attitude.

Activity:

- Share an upsetting feeling with your parents this week.
- Ask a librarian for a book that will teach you more techniques on how to deal with feelings that are upsetting to you.
- Enroll in a karate class to help with self-management.

SUCCESS TIP #38

Take Risks

Do not be afraid to do things that you perceive at the moment to be impossible. Taking risks will pull you away from your comfort zone and to a level you never, in a million years, thought you could reach. This creates a healthier outlook on life. Each risk brings a higher level of consciousness. It exposes the areas in your life that needs improvement. It provides a great way to measure the level of faith that you have in yourself.

Activity:

· Make a decision to take two new risks this week.

· Practice being more self-confident this week.

· Share your results with someone special.

SUCCESS TIP #39

Stop Worrying

Worrying takes up a lot of brainpower. Worrying about a problem or situation shuts down the brain and makes it very hard to find a solution. Without a solution, your worrying could linger on for days or weeks. Simply speak frankly to yourself, and communicate that the problem or issue is only temporary; then begin your breathing exercises or start an action-oriented activity that will take your mind off your worries.

Another way to overcome worry is to assign one day per week as your worry day. This is where all you do is worry (example, Mondays from 5–6pm). When an issue arises that makes you feel like worrying, write it down on a cue card and put it away in a safe place. When your worry day arrives, pull out all your cue cards, and begin worrying for 5–10 minutes each. You will notice that all your problems have disappeared before your "worry day" arrives, which will eliminate your need to worry on that day altogether.

Activity:

- Create a list of things that worries you.
- Pull your list out on your worry day (Mondays from 5:00pm–6:00pm.)
- Give each item on your list equal worrying time.
- Write down your results and share with a friend.

SUCCESS TIP #40

Have Fun

Fun should be your foundation before you begin any activity. With a hectic schedule and multiple responsibilities, you are probably thinking there is no way to have fun. Always find a way to add fun to your day. Implementing this simple tip will improve your immune system and limit the amount of sick days you will be absent from school. Learn to enjoy school, home, your friends or just nature. Be happy about your successes and have more fun with **YOU**.

Activity:

- Express the feeling of excitement regarding school this week.
- Express the feeling of love regarding your home/family this week.
- Express the feeling of enthusiasm about your life today.

SUCCESS TIP #41

Improve Your Memory

Skipping meals will not increase mental power or keep teens healthy. Participating in the weekly diet craze will not improve memory. In order to concentrate better during the day, our mind and body must be in top condition. This means having a balanced nutrition program in place that will nourish the mind, to bring about the results we are looking for. Visit the school nurse to find out more information on the kinds of foods that can and will build brainpower. Start a chart to track the types of foods that increase memory power.

Activity:

- Have more fish, veggies and fruits for breakfast this week.
- Give up all junk food/sweets before noon this week.
- Drink six to eight glasses of water everyday.

SUCCESS TIP #42

Take Time Out

As a teenager, you may find yourself overwhelmed with homework, chores, projects, relationships, a full or part-time job and many other things that take up your time. My recommendation is to schedule a time-out.

Start small and increase your time based on your personal needs. Use this personal time-out to reflect, relax, meditate, smell the roses or give a listening ear to someone else, **YOU**. The idea here is to do what empowers you as an individual. This technique will help to improve both your mental and spiritual abilities.

Activity:

- Choose and label one day weekly as "My Special Day."
- Spend an hour alone this week feeding the ducks.
- Draw a picture of how you see yourself.
- Write about your feelings in your success journal.

SUCCESS TIP #43

Smile

Smiling releases positive energy and healing to the whole body. Smiling can also bring joy to others. It creates a sense of happiness. Happy teens always display big beautiful smiles. Teens with beautiful smiles possess the power to disarm those who are grumpy and unhappy. Smiling reflects the inside of the individual. It tells others that you love, respect and care about yourself. It's a sure sign of a successful teenager.

Activity:

- Give out one hundred **Smiles** today.
- Draw a "Smiley Face" in your success journal today.
- Write a poem about the power of your smile.

SUCCESS TIP #44

Accept Criticism Without Feeling Threatened

It is not worth the headache to take criticism personally. Be willing to listen without having to defend yourself. Criticism is just another way for others to expose their beliefs and/or personal development. Often, it is truthful information regarding the individual doing the criticizing. Remember that you are only reflecting what they are refusing to see in themselves. There is no need to feel threatened. Ignore them and claim victory.

Activity:

- Share this tip with someone who criticizes you this week.
- Say "Something Nice" to all those who criticize you this week.
- Share the results with a parent.

SUCCESS TIP #45

Be Confident In Everything You Do

Be confident with your studies, your daily activities, and your relationships. The higher your level of confidence when you begin a task or relationship, the more likely you will experience success. Many teenagers who have difficulty with friends, school, parents, and simple day-to-day responsibilities do not have a strong level of confidence in themselves, or their personal abilities. Having confidence in yourself is like having faith in your ability to create your own success. Know from the bottom of your heart that you are a successful teenager. Now begin behaving like a successful teenager.

Activity:

- Spend ten minutes reflecting on areas where you have completely let yourself down.

- Remind yourself that you are worthy of success and refuse to accept this behavior.

- Share your breakthrough with a parent or your doctor.

SUCCESS TIP #46

Eliminate Procrastination

Procrastination begins with a little lie that many teenagers tell themselves about accomplishing a task, completing school assignments or chores at home. Many teens tell themselves that they will get to their homework in a 'few minutes,' 'an hour' or even 'tomorrow.' Before you know it, that little lie kept on growing and the homework never got done.

Procrastination is another way for many teens to buy into the belief, that the low grade they received on their last test had nothing to do with the twelve hours spent on the phone during the week, or the sixteen hours spent watching music videos. The best way to get rid of procrastination is to stop LYING! Successful teens take responsibility with all assignments and create deadlines to keep on track.

Activity:

- Look up the word procrastination.
- Create a list of things that you are procrastinating about.
- Set a deadline for completion for each item.
- Share your results with your parents.

SUCCESS TIP #47

Accept No Limitations In Life

Refuse any behavior that is a substitute for what you truly want. If you are a "D" student and you desire to become an "A" student, do not settle. Get a tutor, spend more time studying, start an exercise program, check your eating and sleeping habits, re-evaluate your environment and routine until you can get that "A." Refuse limitations. Your goal is to experience your teenage life without limits of succeeding.

Activity:

- Ask a parent to help with identifying your personal limitations.
- Ask all your teachers for recommendations to improve your grades.
- Ask your friends to do this exercise with you.

SUCCESS TIP #48

Find Out Your Purpose In Life

One of my greatest concerns is for teenagers who go through high school and college, spending hours researching, studying, without knowing what their purpose is in life. Begin as early as possible to develop your true purpose. A true purpose always empowers others not just yourself. It might change, as you get older, but begin now to focus on what your major role is on the planet. This simple act will cut down on any feelings of anxiety or worry as you strive to become more successful each day.

Activity:

- Create a list of things that you are passionate about.
- Choose five from your list that you would like to learn more about.
- Contact three from your list to inquire about volunteering.
- Choose one from your list to volunteer your time monthly.
- Continue this procedure until you develop a passion for living.
- This is your purpose in life.

SUCCESS TIP #49

Begin A Teen Success Journal

Starting a success journal will definitely improve your skills to become a successful teenager. Use your journal as your personal bible that will help with reaching your maximum potential year after year. Begin by writing down your daily goals, purpose, action-plans, prayer and accomplishments. Your journal can also be used as a reminder of how successful you already are.

My recommendation with journals is to reread them at the end of every month just to get an idea of where you are actually heading. Develop your very own personal library with annual teen success journals. This is an excellent way to chart your life.

Activity:

• Start an annual teen success journal today.

• Record your daily goals, purpose, actions, prayer and accomplishments.

• Share this idea with a friend.

SUCCESS TIP #50

Stay Focused On Your Goals

A recent survey by the Brooks & Brooks Foundation, Inc., showed that teens with written down goals were ten times more likely to succeed, than teens that did not write their goals down. Refuse to accept anything less than the best from yourself on a daily basis. Eliminate excuses as to why you did not write your goals down or why you did not begin a teen success journal. Push yourself to be the best at every assignment, project and relationship. Learn to stay focused on your goals, and expect only good things from yourself.

Activity:

- Create a one, three and five year goals chart.
- Create two or more goals and an action plan for the following areas (education, dreams, social, family, financial, community, spiritual, health)
- Review your goals for each area daily
- Amazing results are awaiting you
- Get started!

Section Three

Education Success Tips

I believe that education is the key to success. This is why educational goals should be in place before beginning high school. It is very important for all teenagers to develop the desire to go beyond high school with their education. Teenagers who acquire more than just a high school diploma, usually has a higher income potential as adults.

In order to obtain your dreams of attending college you will need to start creating a general support system that may include parents, guardians, friends or anyone who will help support your educational dreams and goals of going to college.

Your academic counselor is an excellent source to contact about your current classes, grades, and your overall G.P.A. While, getting good grades in regular classes are great! Getting them in Advanced Placement classes are even better. Remember that maintaining good grades now will help you to get into the college of your choice.

SUCCESS TIP #51

Get Excited About Learning

Acquiring new skills and learning new lessons will aid in building stronger and powerful leadership qualities for the future. Challenge yourself to learn about a subject that you had a small interest in. Learn to be a student of knowledge. Read about projects and books that will elevate your mind and balance your teenage years. Be excited about your studies this year.

Activity:

- Register for a college prep class.
- Participate in a ten-week leadership training class.
- Ask your school counselor for assistance.

SUCCESS TIP #52

Daily Results Equal Personal Actions

Our daily actions produce a negative or positive result. Whether you desire to become class president or start your own tutoring program, the amount and type of energy that is put into these projects will decide your outcome. Lack of action will produce negative results. Waking up late for school, being ungrateful to your parents, turning in assignments after the deadline are behaviors that will produce negative results. Being responsible will produce positive results. Completing homework assignments on time, and turning them in, always produces good grades. Being irresponsible will delay the positive result of becoming a successful teenager.

Activity:

• Keep a very close eye on where you lost energy this week. (Is it in procrastination? Is it in being impatient?)

• Replace all negative behaviors with a positive action this week.

• Record your results in your success journal.

SUCCESS TIP #53

Discover Your Hidden Talents And Strengths

Many successful teens create a list of their strengths and talents in a teen success journal. The journal is then used as a reminder of the many successful tools available to use in class, at home or with friends. Use your talents and strengths to help those who are less fortunate. Share them with others. Conduct a survey to find out what others think your strengths and talents are. You might be surprised. Use this information to improve your overall self-image.

Activity:

- Use your strengths to help someone in need this week.
- Volunteer your talents at a local children's hospital or a non-profit organization.
- Create a list of strengths and talents you would like to develop in the future.

SUCCESS TIP #54

Commit To Being A Successful Teenager

One of the main reasons for experiencing success this year, and in the future, will be based on your level of commitment and work invested for self-development. It is important to put a program in place that shows weekly, monthly and yearly progress. It is impossible to have success without proper planning. Begin working on your high school or college plans immediately. It is your right to achieve success.

Activity:

- Begin a success journal this week.
- Expect to have healthy friendships.
- Expect to do excellent in school.
- Expect to go to college/university.
- Expect to have abundance.
- Commit to win.

SUCCESS TIP #55

Begin A Personal Library

Starting a personal library will help to increase personal knowledge. Your personal library is one of the tools you've used so far to help with becoming a successful teenager. Your grades today reflect your personal library. Invest in personal knowledge and begin your personal library today.

Activity:

- Ask your parent to pick up a bookshelf for your personal library.
- Add one-two books monthly in the area of teen finance, success strategies, study skills, college prep, and self-improvement.
- Attend a book fair to check out the variety of books available for teens.

SUCCESS TIP #56

Do Not Wait For Others To Help You, Help Yourself!

Many teenagers get tired of waiting for help that does not stimulate their ability to learn. Successful teens are now implementing their own solutions to problems, which eliminates waiting until someone comes along to show them how to become a success or to receive information needed in order to complete homework/assignments.

Successful teens are now learning how to be more motivated with their schoolwork. According to surveys completed by Brooks & Brooks Foundation, Inc., successful teens get up early, set a schedule, and create a plan for the day. Teens that begin the day by taking full responsibility for all actions become more skillful and increase learning abilities at an alarming rate.

Activity:

- Purchase a To Do List calendar.
- Write down daily/weekly goals.
- Check off completed goals/assignments.
- Attend a seminar on goal setting at your local library.
- Reward yourself for completing these activities.

SUCCESS TIP #57

Invest Quality Time In Your Homework

Your homework or research time should be a special moment to improve on the subject at hand. With this in mind, hang up the telephone, turn off the television, and put yourself in an environment where you have peace and quiet to complete your homework. The time you invest in your homework always shows up in your final grade, so make it count!

Activity:

- Make a commitment to work ahead of your class this week.
- Complete all essays and assignments and turn them in one week before the due date.
- Get a tutor for weak subjects.

SUCCESS TIP #58

Listen Carefully

Listening skills are necessary for a successful teenager. The most powerful and successful individuals are those who listen attentively to everyone. Do not be a "know it all" teenager. Encourage others to share ideas and thoughts that could eventually make a positive difference in your life.

Do not allow yourself to become the "class clown" or someone who needs so much attention that they dominate every conversation. Teens who listen carefully cut down on study time, and have lots of time left over to complete assignments and still have plenty of time for fun activities.

Activity:

- Practice not interrupting others before they complete a sentence.
- Listen sometimes without taking notes.
- Become more powerful by asking others to share information about their day.

SUCCESS TIP #59

Look Out For Opportunities

Be aware of opportunities that make a positive difference in your life. Opportunities come daily; the key is to get ready to receive. Some opportunities can come from your parents, friends, teachers or mentors. Many of theses opportunities can be used as a teaching tool, such as; how to improve grades, how to get a better job, how to earn more money, or how to maintain balance in life. Be prepared everyday to receive the opportunities coming your way; you never know when the one you've been waiting for will arrive.

Activity:

- Give someone an opportunity today.
- Assist your best friend with a project that he/she is struggling with.
- Assist your teacher with cleaning up after class.

SUCCESS TIP #60

Become Teachable

All truly successful teenagers have had to learn how to become more teachable in order to achieve success. The same is true for you. Many teens repeat the same negative behaviors over and over again only because they have not learned how to become teachable.

I myself struggled with this tip throughout my teenage years, until I decided that it was time for me to move to the next level of becoming more successful. Once I made this decision, I then worked very hard at listening carefully to colleagues who gave me excellent advice about projects and situations, whereas before I refused to listen, because it was my life, and no one understood me enough to tell me what to do.

Activity:

- Take the advice from your parents more seriously.
- Allow others to speak the truth without becoming defensive.
- Learn from your mistakes.

SUCCESS TIP #61

Start Your Day With Intention

Many teenagers start their day off with unbelievable stress. A typical morning for most teens includes, rushing out of bed, inability to find necessary books for class, lots of sugar for breakfast, and a very intense conversation on their cell phone, all before making it to school.

Successful teenagers start their days off with intention. They usually make a plan the night before and therefore create positive intentions for the full day. Successful teens intend to wake up on time, have all their books and assignments in order, have plenty of time for breakfast, and get to school with lots of time left over to socialize with friends before going to class. Teenagers who start their days with intentions usually have greater success with their future.

Activity:

- Spend time tonight to plan tomorrow with intention.
- Ask a parent or mentor for guidance.
- Celebrate your ability to acquire another successful skill.

SUCCESS TIP #62

Become A Teenager That Leads

Learn to lead in an area that shows off your leadership skills. For example, if you are good at math, push yourself to become the math leader in class. If you are good at sports, do the same. You may also find that one of your leadership abilities could be a good listener or good friend. Whatever it may be, train yourself to lead in activities that will enhance your own growth. Become a leader in whatever you feel comfortable doing.

Activity:

- Commit to leadership this week.
- Lead in an activity of your choice.
- Mentor a friend this week.

SUCCESS TIP #63

Do Not Steal

There is a growing concern about teenagers who steal information from computers and sell it to their friends. This is not an attribute of a successful teenager. Stealing occurs when an individual wrongfully takes an item that does not belong to him/her with the intention of selling the stolen item. Copying from your friends at test time is also a form of stealing. Showing up for a test unprepared and using it as an excuse to copy answers from others will not look good on your transcript. Study hard, complete your homework, listen in class and stop stealing.

Activity:

- Spend quality time on your homework.
- Research reports about teenagers who cheat and the consequences.
- Share this tip with friends who copy answers from you at test time.

SUCCESS TIP #64

Manage Your Time Well

Manage your time with care. Eliminate "time wasters" and stay focus on the goals for the day. By managing time effectively, you will find that a lot more things get accomplish, with extra time left over for play. Teens must be conscious of time given to others, whose goal is to take energy.

Teenagers who waste time, usually take away quality time from those who forget to plan their day with intention. Be on guard as to how much time you give to anything that waste time, such as; television, computer or cell phone. Watching the future of others for countless hours on television, or playing games on the computer should not be a replacement for an activity. These are "time wasters," that if not managed well, will affect your progress towards becoming a successful teenager.

Activity:

- Limit television time to only two hours this week.
- Limit video game time to only one hour this week.
- Limit phone time to three hours this week.
- Replace your time with a physical activity: such as basketball with a friend, swimming, jogging, chess, soccer, etc.

SUCCESS TIP #65

Start Your Own Tutoring Program

Many teenagers have a hard time with subjects that can be difficult. This is a great opportunity to begin a teen tutoring program that will help others, and provide an opportunity of a part-time job. A teen tutoring program can be very simple. Teens can work one hour weekly with a single client or work ten hours weekly with a group of clients. Teens can also tutor in one subject or more. Teens interested in starting a tutoring business in their community should check with local authorities about rules and regulations, and write a one-page business plan before receiving payment from clients.

Activity:

- Start a Teen Tutoring Business.
- Check out books at your local library on how to start a teen business.
- Write a one-page business plan.
- Seek out a mentor who owns an existing business.

SUCCESS TIP #66

Become A Speaker On Campus

Being a successful teenager means that your peers are interested in how and what you are doing that makes you a success. One of the ways you can share your success with others is by becoming a speaker in an area that you love most. It could be about algebra, community improvement, science or history, as long as it is a subject that you love talking about and that can also benefit others.

Activity:

- Offer a thirty-minute free seminar on your best subject.
- Volunteer your speaking abilities to a school or church activity.
- Write and publish a book about your success strategies.

SUCCESS TIP #67

Make A Commitment To Excel

Make a commitment to yourself that no matter what it takes, no matter how hard you have to work, no matter how many times you fail; you will push yourself to succeed in life. This is a necessary requirement for all successful teenagers.

Activity:

- Write down a list of one hundred dreams that you would like to experience before graduating college.
- Begin an action plan for each dream.
- Check off each dream upon completion.

SUCCESS TIP #68

Read Motivational And Inspirational Books

Allow time for reading/listening to inspirational or motivational material that deal with teen self-development. Reading or listening to these materials will inspire you to become your best. This behavior produces a healthy mind. There are many materials available at your local bookstore, and library. School counselors are another great resource you can use to assist in acquiring a list of motivational and inspirational books for teens.

Activity:

- Visit your local library.
- Ask the librarian to show you a listing of motivational and inspirational books for teenagers.
- Complete an application for a library card.
- Begin checking out your favorite books regularly.
- Visit your school counselor for more information.

SUCCESS TIP #69

Allow Yourself To Make Mistakes

Making mistakes is an opportunity for greatness. Mistakes are there to assist with becoming stronger, wiser and better. Mistakes are there to show just how mentally, physically and spiritually strong we are. When we allow ourselves to make mistakes, we are simply giving ourselves another chance at becoming more successful.

Activity:

- Create a list of mistakes that you have made within the past month.
- Write down your reaction next to each mistake.
- Take a look at your list to see which ones made you stronger and wiser.
- Share this with a teacher.

SUCCESS TIP #70

Improve Your Area Of Excellence

Each of us has one or more areas that we excel in, but no matter how well we do in a particular area, there is always room for improvement. Spend time researching how you can bring your level of excellence to a point where it will make a difference not only for yourself, but for others as well.

Activity:

- Spend time this week sharing one of your exceptional skills with a friend.
- Ask your friend to do the same with you.
- Record the results in your success journal.

SUCCESS TIP #71

Expect Things To Work Out Well

It may seem difficult to put all of these lessons into action, especially when you do not know whether or not they will work for you. This is an excellent time to see just how much you have learned so far. Give yourself credit and expect that all the work you have done so far will only produce good results. If the results are not good enough, simply re-adjust your plans until you are implementing the activities that will aid in getting the results you are looking for.

Activity:

- Practice the art of expecting goodness in a difficult task today.
- Ask a mentor to guide you with a difficult task this week.
- Share results with a friend.

SUCCESS TIP #72

Practice Self-Discipline

An ingredient for failure is lack of self-discipline. Teens who lack self-discipline tend to blame others for their problems instead of taking responsibility for their situation; these individuals usually find excuses as to why a project did not get completed, and allow themselves to wallow in self-pity while asking "why is this happening to me?" Begin today to take full charge of your life. Discipline yourself to become more responsible, and overcome procrastination. Eliminate blaming others and deal with the consequences when you have messed up.

Activity:

- Share this tip with someone who complains all the time.
- Become a mentor to a friend who always blames others for his/her problem.
- Reward yourself for the ability to share positive resources with your friends.

SUCCESS TIP #73

Evaluate Your Progress

At the end of each week or month, go over all you have done. Go over your goals and your time-management list. Go over your mission statement. Evaluate your level of progress; look at where you started to get a better idea of where you are heading. Take this tip very serious it could save your life.

Activity:

- Review your five-year goals list today to see if you are on track.
- Create a monthly checkpoint to evaluate your progress.
- Feel free to make changes.

SUCCESS TIP #74

Always Ask For Help

Successful teenagers refuse to begin a project or an exam without being fully prepared to give their best. Ask for help ahead of time so that you will be prepared to produce your best work. It takes courage and high self-esteem to ask for help. All teenagers have the ability to ask. Do not settle with an "OK" behavior. Respect yourself enough to know that you can do better and that you will put forth an effort in asking someone for help before it's too late.

Activity:

- Participate in a study group this week.
- Ask lots of questions this week.
- Visit your school counselor to request scholarship information.
- Start a teen club this month teaching other students how to implement the tips you learned from reading this book.

SUCCESS TIP #75

Seek To Become Wise

Happy is the teen that is wise and successful. Acquiring wisdom should be at the top of the list of leadership skills for all successful teens. Teens who live life guided by wisdom will not fail, stumble, or fall when it comes time to be tested for other levels of success. Be strong! Eliminate the fear to become a wise and successful teenager.

Activity:

- Create a list of wise teens and adults.
- Choose four from your list and research individuals.
- Select two from your research to approach for possible mentorship.

Section Four

Social Success Tips

Socializing for teens is a priority every day. I believe that teens would be very happy if the amount of time spent in school were exchanged with the amount of time spend socializing.

Many teens are good at the game of socializing and others are not, but it is very interesting to just watch how the game is played and see who wins the popularity contest each day, because it changes. There are new players added and removed every day from this active game that does not need permission to be enlisted.

I was a very shy teen growing up, so I did not enjoy this game very much. I must say that I did learn how to rely and trust myself more because there was no one there for me, so I thought! Being shy and not knowing how to express myself pushed many people away. As I got older, I learned how to be friendlier, and in turn reaped a harvest of friendships that I am very proud to have. It took a while, but I am glad that I never gave up.

The success tips in this section are meant to release personal power and give teens the permission to allow others to be themselves. I encourage teenagers to enjoy all friendships, no matter how short, how long or even sometimes confusing. The experience of being in a relationship will also help to build character and leadership skills for the future. This is more important than being unfriendly. Give yourself a chance and get in the game!

SUCCESS TIP #76

Do Not Envy Others

Envying others for their ability to get good grades without studying, or for their ability to have lots of friends is not an attribute of a successful teenager. All teenagers are blessed with everything they need in order to succeed in life. At times it might look like others are doing better than you, but look closer, and you will find that your life is just as great, sometimes better.

Many teenagers experience lack due to the fact that they are too busy envying others. When teens wish bad for others, they set themselves up to lose their blessings. Teens with envy push opportunities away, and spend many years trying to find out why their big break has not arrived. Teens should develop the habit of blessing other teens. Teens should wish success for other teens. Successful teenagers enjoy helping, mentoring, and sharing their skills with others, not envying.

Activity:

- Bless as many teens possible this week.
- Say good things about others, when you see them with what you desire.
- Share this tip with other teens.

SUCCESS TIP #77

Accept People For Who They Are

When an individual makes a nasty comment about his/herself, believe it and accept it. Do not expect others to treat you better than the way they treat themselves. By building strong self-esteem and personal confidence, you will grow to realize that it is better to accept people for who they really are, which will eliminate having to ask yourself the question "how could he/she do that to me?"

Activity:

- Take note of others who disrespect you.
- Do not try to change them.
- Begin immediately to honor yourself more.
- Change how you communicate to yourself.
- Look around to see just how much your reflection has changed.
- If you are not happy with your results, continue to honor yourself at a higher level.

SUCCESS TIP #78

Change Your Association

Successful teenagers understand clearly that they need to choose healthy associations because it could bring life or death. Many teenagers hang around individuals who drink alcohol, smoke, commit crimes, and use violence, just to belong to the group. This type of association has brought many disappointing phone calls from the police to parents who had no idea about his/her child's associations.

Be a wise teen and choose your associations with care. If you are currently linked to negative associations, ask your mentor for ways to help with changing your association.

Activity:

• Write down a list of activities that you engage in with your friends.

• Ask yourself "Would my parents approve of my friends/associates?"

• Introduce your parents to all members in your group.

SUCCESS TIP #79

Allow Others To Be Responsible For Themselves

Refuse to take on the responsibilities of others. Allow others to learn new skills, improve their behavior and make their own mistakes so that they, too, can become a success at whatever they choose to do.

If you are always willing to complete your friends' homework, solve all their problems or take the rap for something they have done, you are lowering your self-worth and making it easier for that individual to fail at life. It is much easier to give support by recommending books, tapes, seminars or an ear that will aid in helping this individual cope or deal with his or her own issues in a positive way.

Activity:

- Practice tough love with your friends this week.
- Recommend a book to a friend who is troubled.
- Refer a troubled friend to one of your mentors this week.

SUCCESS TIP #80

Surround Yourself With Positive People

It is very important in today's society for teens to become and stay more positive. It is way too easy to become negative. Surrounding yourself with positive people will motivate you towards achieving your dream of becoming a doctor or lawyer in the future. It will cut down on the negative self-talk, and will establish an excellent resource to reach out to when you are in need.

Activity:

- Create a list of positive people in your life.
- Write down what you like about each person.
- Write down what you like about yourself.
- Share this activity with a friend.

SUCCESS TIP #81

Speak Only Good Things About Others

When you speak well about others you are, in turn, speaking good about yourself. What you say with your mouth always comes back to you in one form or another. What you say with your mouth could be the reason for your success or failure in the future. Become conscious about what you are saying when you are saying it. Become aware of the messages you are sending out. Speak only good things about others and goodness will return to you always.

Activity:

• Catch your friends speaking good things about others and buy them a treat.

• Dare your friends to do the same.

• Share your results with a mentor.

SUCCESS TIP #82

Do Not Covet Your Friends

Get into the habit of being happy for your friends instead of coveting their possessions, family, or their ability to get good grades. Most of the time it looks like your friends and others are living a great life, but you do not know the **PAIN** that they endure sometimes behind closed doors. All you see are the results. When you crave for the things your friends possess, understand that you are also coveting the pain that goes along with it.

Activity:

- Release yourself from envy this week.
- Compliment and bless all your friends this week.
- Refrain from asking where did you get it, and how much did it cost.

SUCCESS TIP #83

Do Not Allow Yourself To Be Victimized

Most teenagers allow negative things to happen over and over again without asserting themselves in a positive way, make it easier to become a victim. This is not a positive way to seek attention from others. Speak up when you are not happy about a situation. You are the only one that knows what is best for you, and what makes you happy. You are also the only one that can give permission, verbally or non-verbally, for others to treat you with disrespect.

Activity:

• Create a list of areas that you allow yourself to be victimized.

• Pick up a book at your local library on how to build strong Self-Esteem.

• Practice some tips from this book "100 Ways."

• Assert yourself positively daily.

SUCCESS TIP #84

Make An Effort To Become A Better Person

Becoming a better person should always be at the top of your list. Working hard and taking control over your day makes it much easier to become a better person. Becoming a better person will bring more happiness, success, peace of mind at home and school. It will help to bring about the results you desire.

Activity:

- Survey your family and friends on ideas for becoming a better person.
- Implement two or more ideas this week.
- Write down your results in your success journal.

SUCCESS TIP #85

Assert Yourself Positively

When someone offends you, it is only right that you assert yourself in a positive way by letting that individual know that they have offended you. Many times we get offended, and wait weeks, months and sometimes years before we let the other person know just how much pain they have caused us. This pain can sometimes develop into many sicknesses.

As time past, the individual that caused the pain has forgotten about the incident. On the other hand, the person who is experiencing the pain have allowed the situation to block themselves from doing things, or going to their favorite places. Many teens practice this unhealthy behavior only when they have failed to stand up for themselves. Asserting yourself positively will force the other person to take responsibility for their behavior, and allow you to have a clear head to study and sleep at night.

Activity:

- Take an Assertive Training Class.
- Practice letting people know immediately when they offend you.
- Stand up for yourself this week.

SUCCESS TIP #86

Practice Self-Control

Remember that no one owes you anything in life. I encourage all teenagers to practice self-control with their thoughts, behavior and attitude. Self-control is a powerful leadership skill, that when acquired can bring great respect and honor. Successful teens will not draw attention to themselves by displaying lack of self-control. Teens who act up in class or bully other teens are only showing the world that they need someone to care and love them more.

Activity:

- Create a list of things that you have difficult time controlling.
- Spend five minutes creating a positive image for each item.
- Share this tip with a friend who is out of control.

SUCCESS TIP #87

Join A Club

Teens can improve their lives by simply joining a social club that will expose them to different cultures or activities that are of interest. Social clubs at time can provide a safe place where teens can open up and learn to communicate with individuals with the same or even different interests from various backgrounds. Participating in this activity is an excellent way to build stronger social skills. Learn to have fun interacting with positive and motivated teens.

Activity:

- Enroll in a social club at school.
- Share your culture with the group.
- Request information about a teen empowerment club in your community.

SUCCESS TIP #88

Reward Yourself

Reward yourself every time you accomplish a task that makes you proud. Go out of your way to do something fun and unusual. This act will immediately send a positive message that will increase self-esteem and boost leadership abilities. A reward could be a new pair of shoes, a hair cut or a new attitude. You are the only one that can decide what your reward should be. It does not have to cost money. It could be spending the day by the ocean, by the lake, or taking a walk only to be at peace.

Activity:

• Put aside an extra ten percent of all money received this month towards your teen financial portfolio.

• Pay off all debt owed to your friends and family.

• Purchase your first stock.

SUCCESS TIP #89

Refuse Personal Neglect

Refuse self-hatred and all attributes that have the ability to destroy your dreams. Refuse personal neglect in any form. Refuse the desire to sabotage your day. Refuse the desire to be unkind to strangers. Refuse to participate at a level that produces negative results. Hold your head up, and recognize your greatness, your power, and worth. Hold your head up and see the results of being a successful teenager.

Activity:

- Spend an extra ten minutes today in positive self-talk.
- Allow yourself to be a little more understanding with your friends today.
- Smile at someone who looks sad this week.

SUCCESS TIP #90

See Yourself As A Success

Visualize yourself as the success you know you can be. Visualize yourself as a confident, strong and powerful teen. The way you perceive yourself sometimes determines how you allow others to treat you. Visualization can be very helpful for teenagers who struggle with poor self-image. This excellent tool can be used to remove some of the negative things that were spoken into your life by yourself and others. Share your new perception and get involved with people or activities that demonstrate your success. Do not be afraid to accept goodness. You are worth it.

Activity:

- Add a new page in your scrapbook that reflects the success you desire to experience in your lifetime.
- Write out the affirmation "I am a success" ten times today.
- Take your friends for coffee, share your results.

SUCCESS TIP #91

Become The C.E.O. For Your Life

Be the one in charge of what your life's outcome will be. Set up a plan of action for every area of your life. Seek out and acquire mentors for the areas that are important to you. Consult with your mentors monthly for advice and support. Successful teenagers implement and review their plans annually. Take full responsibility for your future and welcome the opportunity to become your very own C.E.O. Take charge of your life's outcome.

Activity:

- Create a committee for your life.
- Select mentors that will help you to succeed.
- Ask your mentors to assist with creating your "Annual Teen Success Scrap Book."
- Meet with your mentors monthly.
- Take your mentors out to celebrate your success.

SUCCESS TIP #92

Make The Choice To Succeed

There will be obstacles along the way to groom and prepare you for life's challenges. It is how you perceive these obstacles that will bring success or failure. Will you perceive your obstacles as a major threat or as an opportunity to improve yourself? Will you perceive doom in everything you do or victory? Your choice to succeed is a gift given to you from birth. The choice to succeed is up to you. Remind yourself daily about the power that lies within you and choose success everyday.

Activity:

- Review your success journals.
- Add pictures and awards of your past and current successes.
- Share your completed journals with a friend.

SUCCESS TIP #93

Stick To Your Plans

Remember, you are already a successful teenager. In order to experience success at it's highest level, one must stick to his/her plans. You may not be as successful as you would like to be today, but by staying on path with your plans, and implementing only a couple of these suggestions you are one-step closer than you were yesterday.

Activity:

- Review your five goals with a friend.
- Spend time developing a detail action plan.
- Repeat this activity if you would like to experience daily successes.

SUCCESS TIP #94

Take Action

Plan out your day to succeed every night before you go to bed. Start the day off with a "plan of action" list. Create a mandatory list of things to complete before the end of the day. Track how and where your time is being spent. Keep track of the amount of time you spend on things that have nothing to do with your goals or mission. Track your social time is it interfering with your studies?

Activity:

- Add up time spent doing homework within the past 24 hours.
- Add up time spent watching television, playing, talking on telephone within past 24 hours.
- Add up time spent slept within past 24 hours.
- Add up time spent at school within the past 24 hours.
- Take a good look at where the majority of your time is being spent.
- Make changes to support your purpose in life.

SUCCESS TIP #95

Become Self-Motivated

Statistics say that most teenagers lack motivation. This can be true for some, but not all. Teenagers find it hard at times, to motivate themselves for success. Some of the areas include; wakening up on time in the morning for school, cleaning their room, and helping with chores around the house. Developing the skill of self-motivation, takes repetitive positive actions that command a change for success. An excellent way to push forward with this tip is to follow through on personal discipline and goals until it becomes a habit.

Activity:

- Write down a list of things you need in order to become more self-motivated.
- Catch yourself being self-motivated and reward yourself every time.
- Share results with a group of friends.

SUCCESS TIP #96

Program Yourself For Success

Successful teens are the only one responsible for the level of success achieved during their lifetime. What you do or do not do today, tomorrow or next year will affect the outcome of your success. Your parents, friends, teachers and relatives are there for guidance and support **only**. It is up to you to take the necessary steps to complete the work that will bring success one-step closer. Successful teenagers must have the desire and the commitment to win at life.

Activity:

• Review your five-year goals list.

• Add one new action per goal.

• Share your results with a mentor.

SUCCESS TIP #97

Explore Ways To Increase Knowledge

Surfing the Internet is a great way to explore ways to increase your knowledge base. There are plenty of interesting topics available online to learn about. Read up on books that will stretch your mind to another dimension. Find other sources such as leadership trainings, DVD's, and educational television programs. Use these resources to help with learning about new ways to become more successful. This success tip can be very empowering for a teen social group. Knowledge is another leadership tool available to all teenagers. Get yours today!

Activity:

- Spend an hour with a grandparent this week (ask them to share stories from their past with you.)
- Look up the definition of the word "Knowledge."
- Write your name next to it.

SUCCESS TIP #98

Set Daily/Weekly Goals

At the beginning of each week set aside time for goal setting. You can begin with weekly goals. When you are comfortable, begin a chart for daily goals. Your goals should be a list of things that you would like to improve in yourself. Set goals to improve your study time, your grades, your personal health, and even your relationships. Make your goals fun, but not too easy. Try making it a game.

Activity:

- Write down a list of twenty goals you would like to experience financially before graduating high school.
- Set a deadline for each goal.
- Check off your goals as you complete them.

SUCCESS TIP #99

Write Out Ten Affirmations Daily

At the beginning of each day, write out ten positive things about yourself. For example, "I, Wendy, am a successful teenager" or "I, Paul, enjoy all my friend-ships." This simple action is just another way of learning how to take daily responsibility. It builds self-esteem and helps to guide teens on the way to becoming the successful teen that everyone adores.

Activity:

- Share one of your affirmations with a friend.
- Ask your friend at the end of the day to give feedback about your behavior.
- Create affirmations for other areas that need improvement.

SUCCESS TIP #100

Look Like A Successful Teenager

Take pride in how you look. Make sure you look and smell your best every day. If you do not like your hair, body or style, try to accept it, then take gradual steps towards improvement. By doing this, you are creating a good "first impression," a teenager who knows and believes that he/she is worthy of success.

Activity:

- Give yourself an elaborate makeover.
- Treat your new look to a new outfit.
- Write us a letter about how this book helped you.

Conclusion

I hoped that this book gave you the motivation and inspiration needed to move towards choosing success on a daily basis. There are many situations in life where these success tips will not apply, so I encourage you to develop your own success tips and add to this list.

I wish that your teenage years be filled with success and wealth. I know and believe that you will take responsibility for all your actions and non-actions. I confess that you will have good health and prosperous relationships with your family and friends. Most of all I declare that with every power within me, you are a successful teenager because of your commitment and dedication in completing this book.

Seminars/Workshops

For additional information on educational programs, books, seminars and lectures by Yvonne Brooks, call 818-623-7332 or send in the coupon below.

_____

Name (Please Print)

_____

Address

_____

City   State   Zip

Please send information on _____ Seminars _____ Lectures
_____Books _____Educational Programs

Mail to:
Yvonne Brooks
6320 Canoga Ave
Suite #1500-123
Woodland Hills, California 91367
818-623-7332

Register your school, organization or church now for one of Yvonne's powerful lecturers.
Email request: ypbrooks@msn.com or call (818) 623-7332

Preparing for High School
And College

FREE Ten-Week Youth Leadership Program

Register now at www.youthleadership3000.org

Or call 818-623-7332

About the Author

Yvonne Brooks is an educator and leadership consultant with over fifteen years of experience. She is the founder and president of the Brooks & Brooks Foundation, Inc., the only non-profit organization that provides a series of FREE Youth Leadership Trainings online, after school and home study to students nationwide.

She provides workshops, seminars, and specialized training programs in a variety of subjects for students, parents, schools, government institutions and businesses. Yvonne is also the creator of the Teen Success Book Series, Financial Planning for Young Adults and Principles for Staying Motivated.

978-0-595-37681-0
0-595-37681-9

Printed in the United States
122124LV00002B/94-102/A